SCHIRMER'S LIBRARY OF MUSICAL CLASSICS

Vol. 2044

JOHANN SEBASTIAN BACH

Collected Transcriptions

26 Piano Transcriptions by
Great Composers and Pianists

For Piano

ISBN 978-0-7935-6810-9

G. SCHIRMER, Inc.

DISTRIBUTED BY

7777 W. BLUEMOUND RD. P.O.BOX 13819 MILWAUKEE, WI 53213

Copyright © 1999 by G. Schirmer, Inc. (ASCAP) New York, NY
International Copyright Secured. All Rights Reserved.
Warning: Unauthorized reproduction of this publication is
prohibited by Federal law and subject to criminal prosecution.

CONTENTS

Aria from Cantata No. 36
    transcribed by Harold Bauer (1873–1951) 1

Chaconne from Sonata for Violin No. 4
    arranged for the left hand by Johannes Brahms (1833–1897) 9
    transcribed by Ferruccio Busoni (1866–1924) 23

Die Seele ruht in Jesu Händen (My Soul Doth Rest in Jesus' Keeping) from Cantata No. 127
    arranged by Harold Bauer 41

Durch Adams Fall ist ganz verderbt (Through Adam Came Our Fall)
    transcribed by Ferruccio Busoni 46

Fantasy and Fugue in G minor
    arranged by Franz Liszt (1811–1886) 50

Gavotte from Sonata for Violin No. 2
    transcribed by Camille Saint-Saëns (1835–1921) 64

Ich ruf zu dir, Herr (I Call on Thee, Lord)
    transcribed by Ferruccio Busoni 68

In dir ist Freude (In Thee is Gladness)
    transcribed by Ferruccio Busoni 70

Jesus bleibet meine Freude (Jesu, Joy of Man's Desiring) from Cantata No. 147
    arranged by Wilhelm Kempff (1895–1991) 74

Komm' süsser Tod (Come, Sweet Death)
    arranged by Harold Bauer 78

Nun freut euch, lieben Christen (Rejoice, Beloved Christians)
    transcribed by Ferruccio Busoni 80

Prelude and Fugue in A minor
    arranged by Franz Liszt 86

Prelude and Fugue in C major
    arranged by Franz Liszt 98

Prelude and Fugue in D major
    transcribed by Ferruccio Busoni 105

Prelude and Fugue (St. Anne's) in E-flat major
    transcribed by Ferruccio Busoni 119

Prelude and Fugue in E minor
    arranged by Franz Liszt 137

Prelude from Partita in E major for Violin
    transcribed by Sergei Rachmaninoff (1873–1943) 153

Prelude to the Ratswahl Cantata
    arranged by Wilhelm Kempff 162

Siciliano from Flute Sonata No. 2
    arranged by Wilhelm Kempff 168

Presto after J.S. Bach
    Johannes Brahms
        First Version 170
        Second Version 174

Toccata and Fugue in C major
    transcribed by Ferruccio Busoni 178

Toccata and Fugue in D minor
    transcribed by Ferruccio Busoni 199

Wachet auf, ruft uns die Stimme (Awake, the Voice Commands)
    transcribed by Ferruccio Busoni 215
    arranged by Wilhelm Kempff 218

ARIA
from Cantata No. 36

Johann Sebastian Bach
transcribed by Harold Bauer

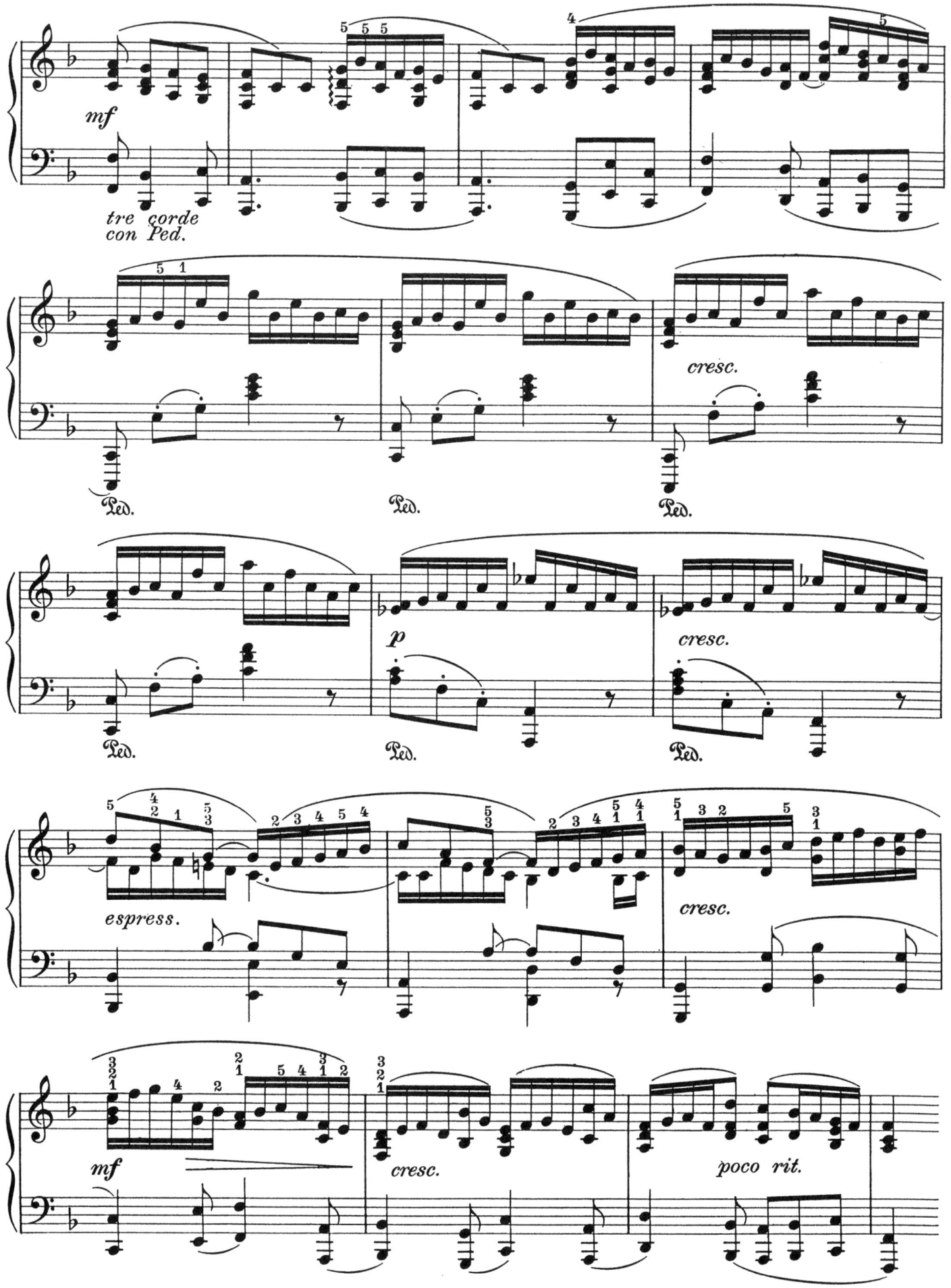

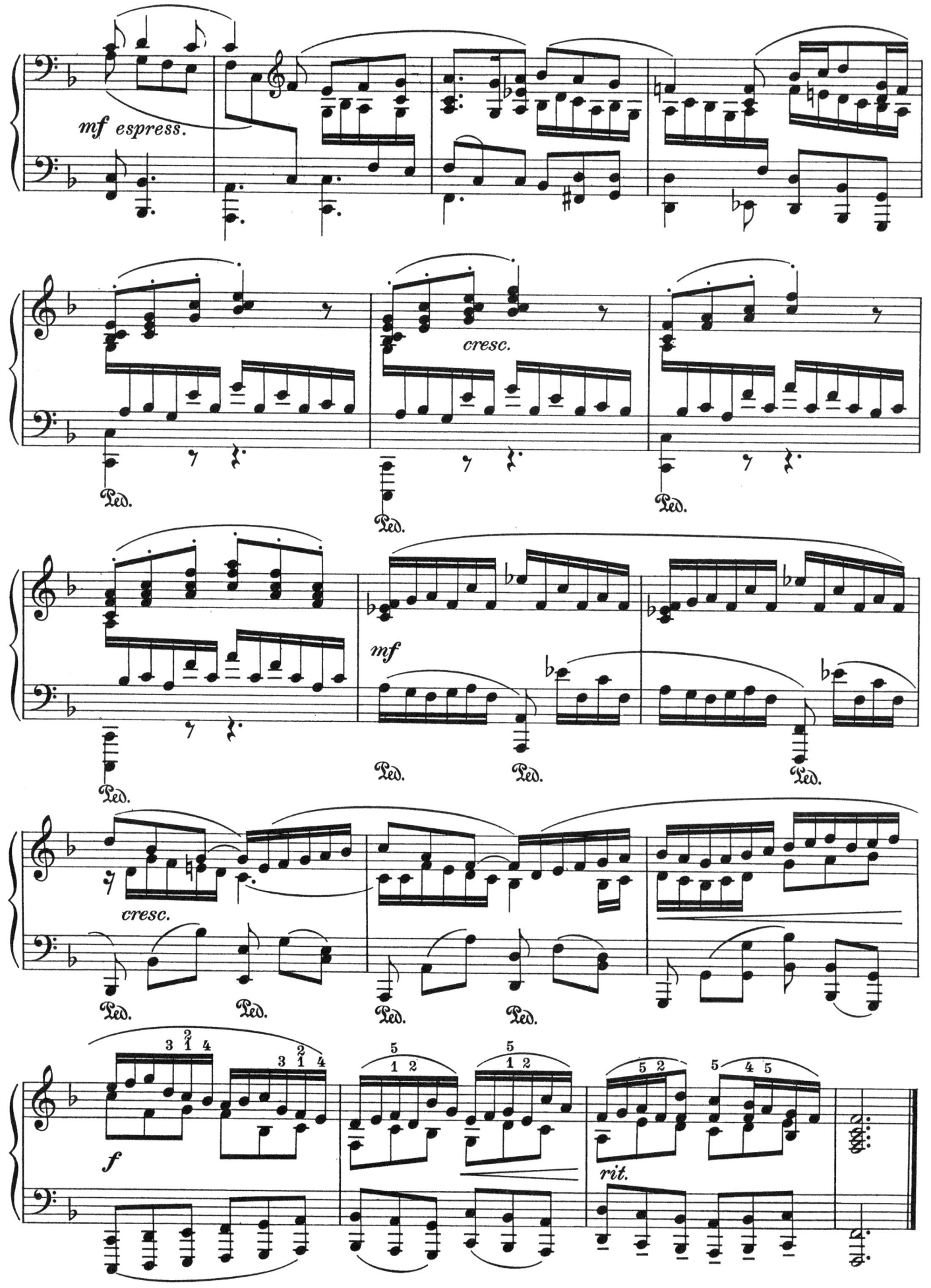

CHACONNE
from Sonata for Violin No. 4

*arranged for the left hand
by Johannes Brahms*

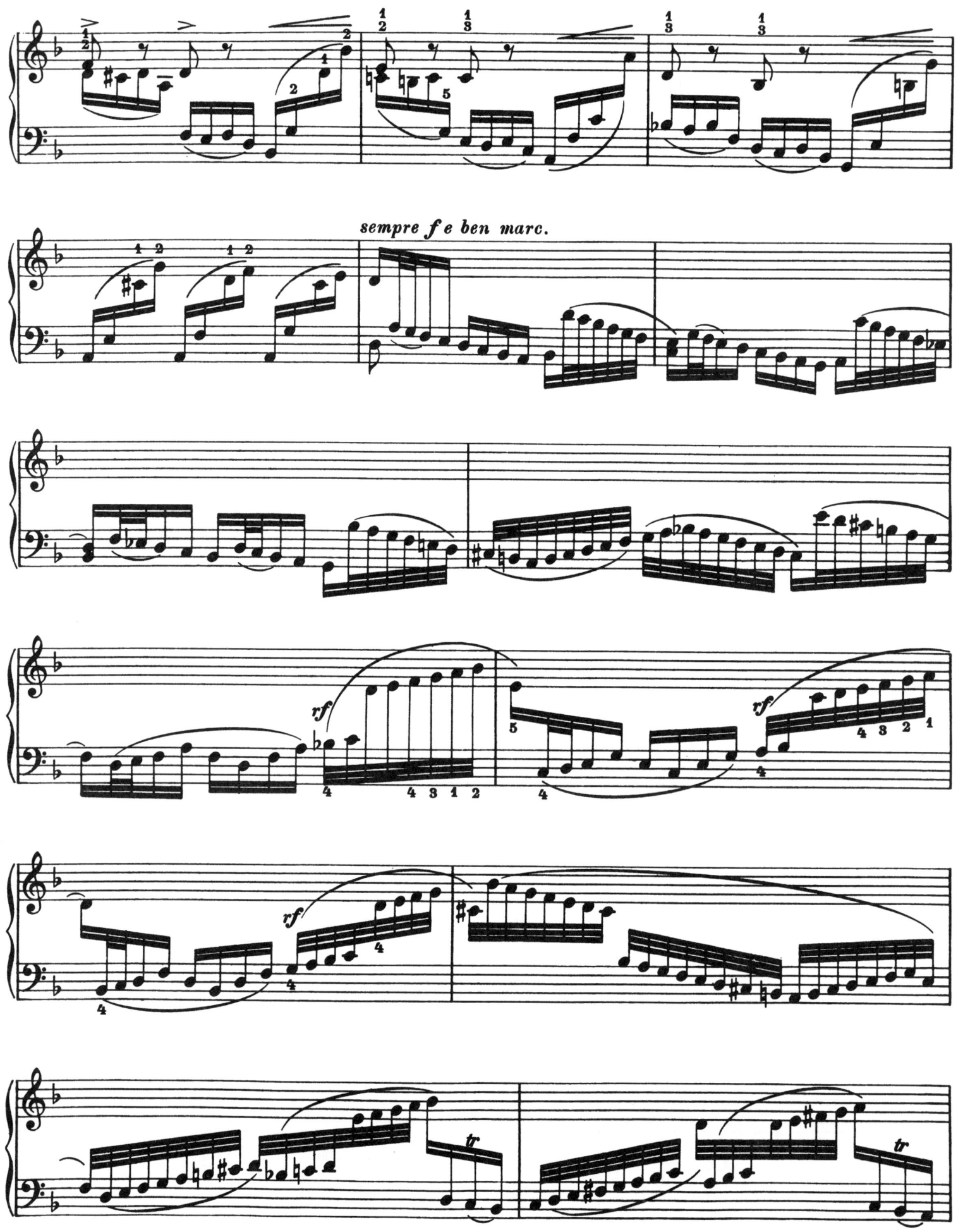

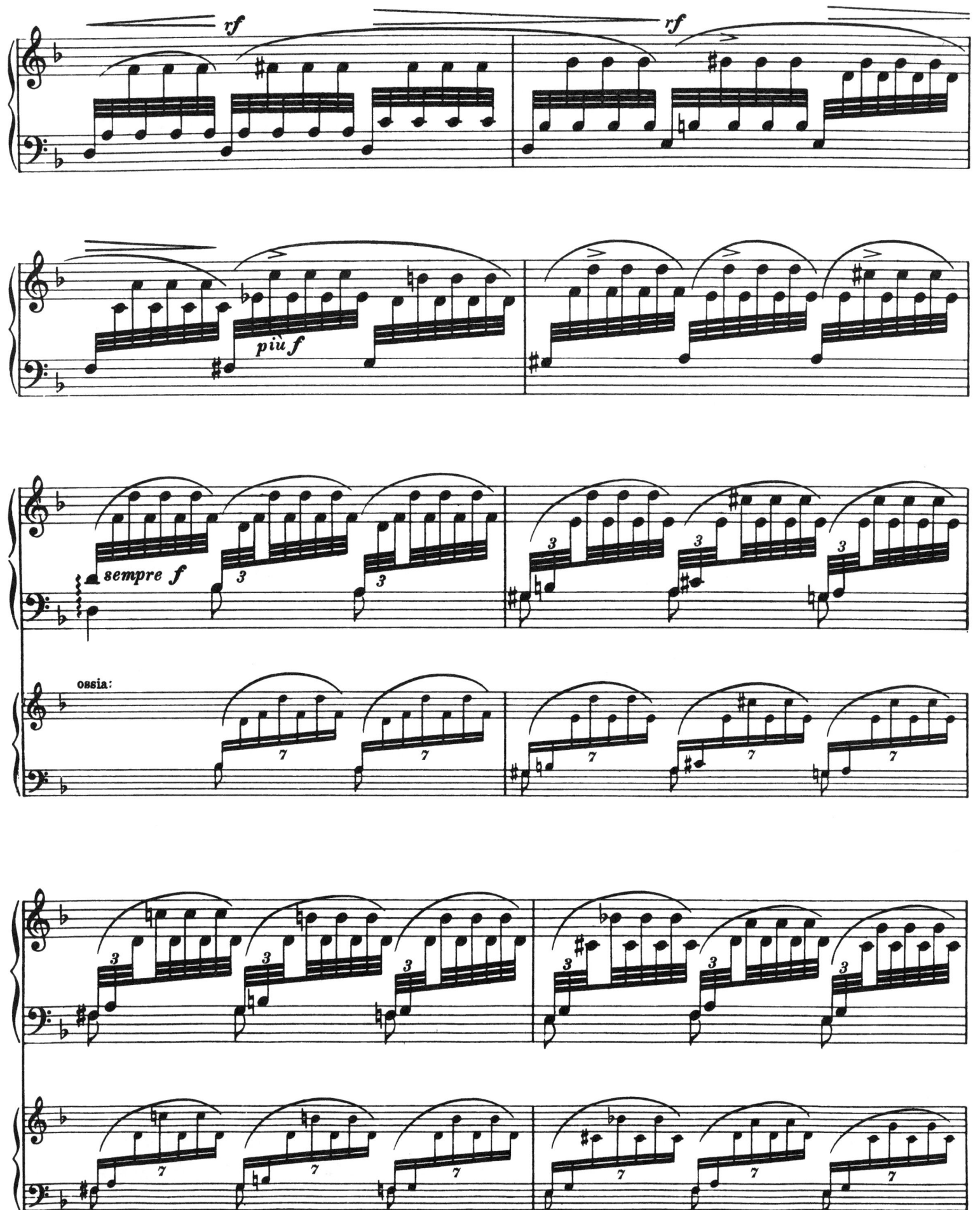

CHACONNE
from Sonata for Violin No. 4

transcribed by Ferruccio Busoni

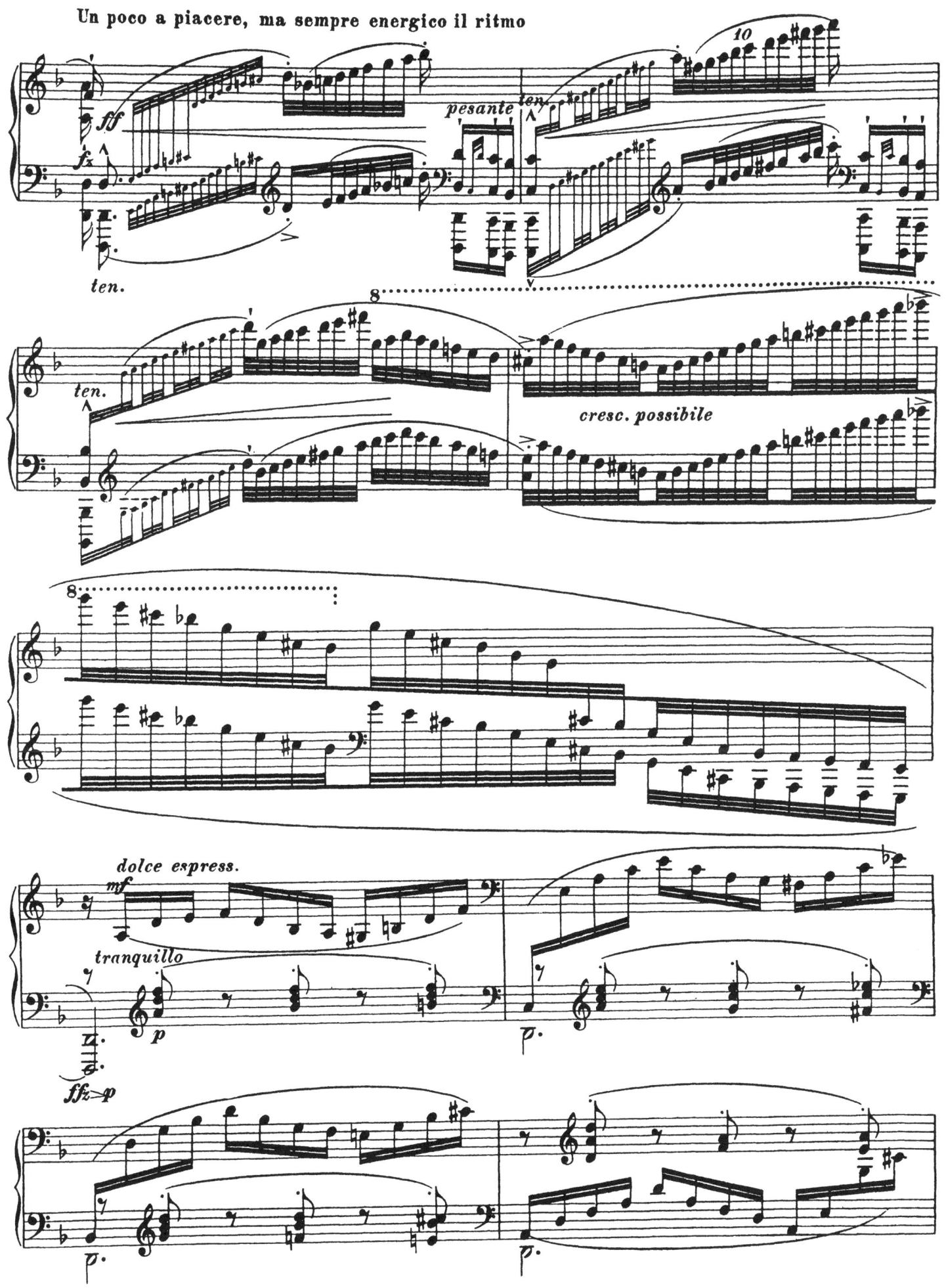

ossia:
martell.
cresc. sempre
più cresc.
cresc. poco a poco
più cresc.
marcato
ossia:
sempre in tempo
ff
allarg.
ff e ritenuto
ff
Più vivo
cresc.
f
mf
marc.

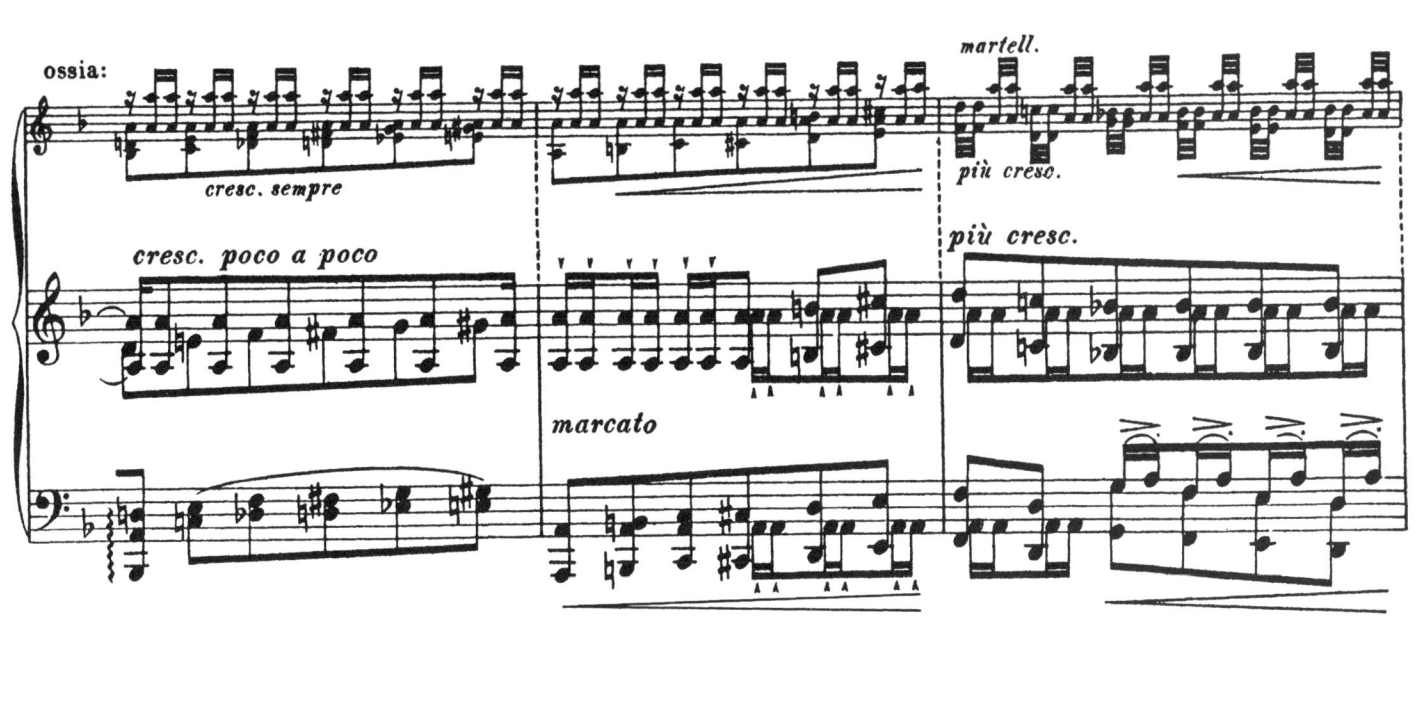

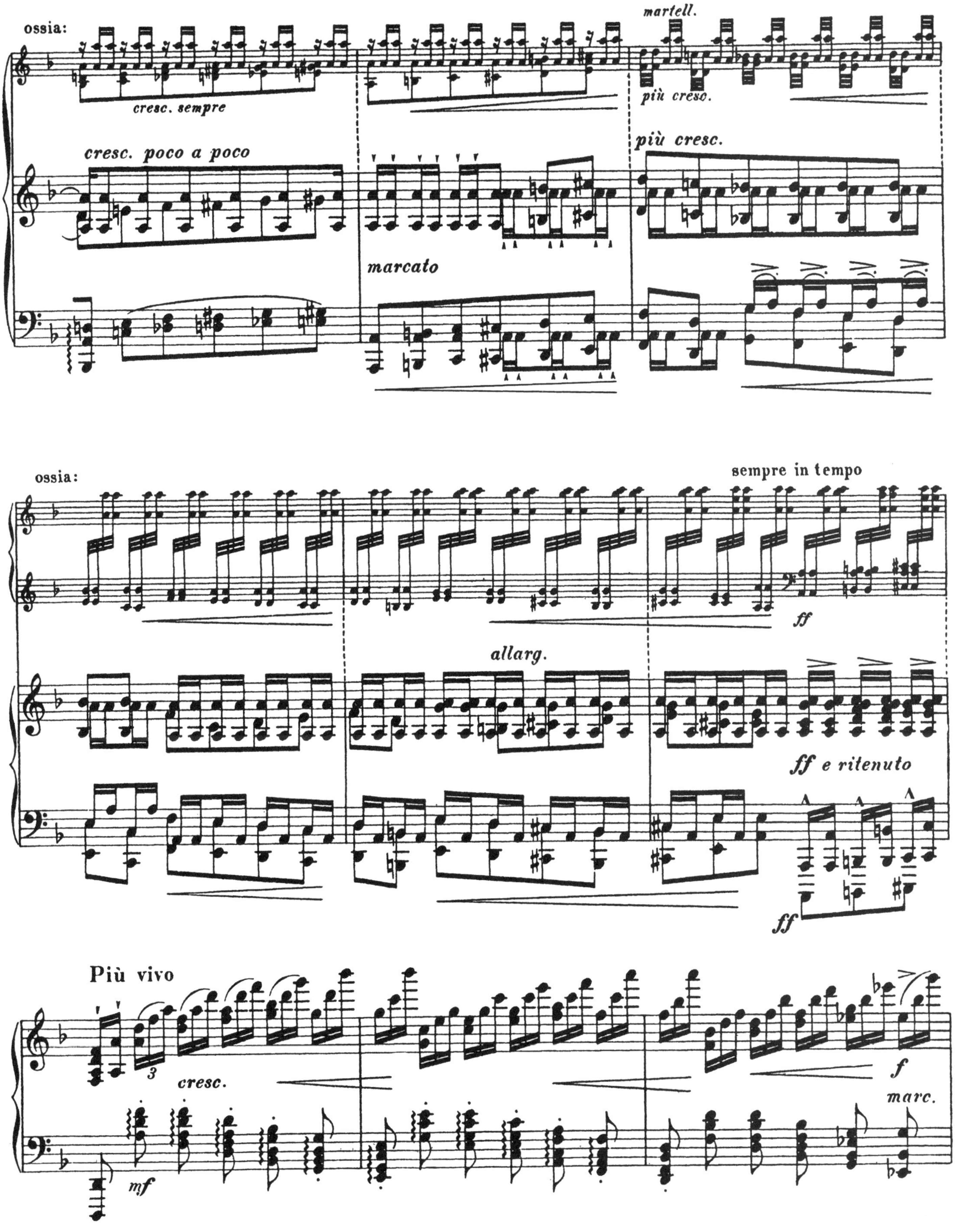

DIE SEELE RUHT IN JESU HÄNDEN
(My Soul Doth Rest in Jesus' Keeping)
from Cantata No. 127

arranged by Harold Bauer

Copyright © 1944 (renewed) by G. Schirmer, Inc. (ASCAP) New York, NY
International Copyright Secured. All Rights Reserved.
Warning: Unauthorized reproduction of this publication is
prohibited by Federal law and subject to criminal prosecution.

DURCH ADAMS FALL IST GANZ VERDERBT
(Through Adam Came Our Fall)

transcribed by Ferruccio Busoni

Fugue[*]

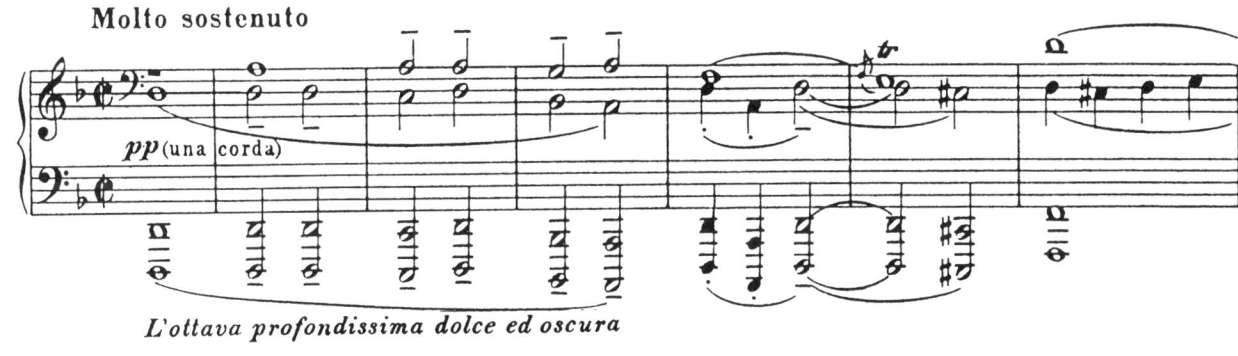

L'ottava profondissima dolce ed oscura

[*] *The preceding piece may serve as immediate prelude to this.*

[**] *The wide stretches must not be played arpeggio.*

an Herrn Professor Sigmund Lebert
FANTASY AND FUGUE
in G minor

Fantasy

arranged by Franz Liszt

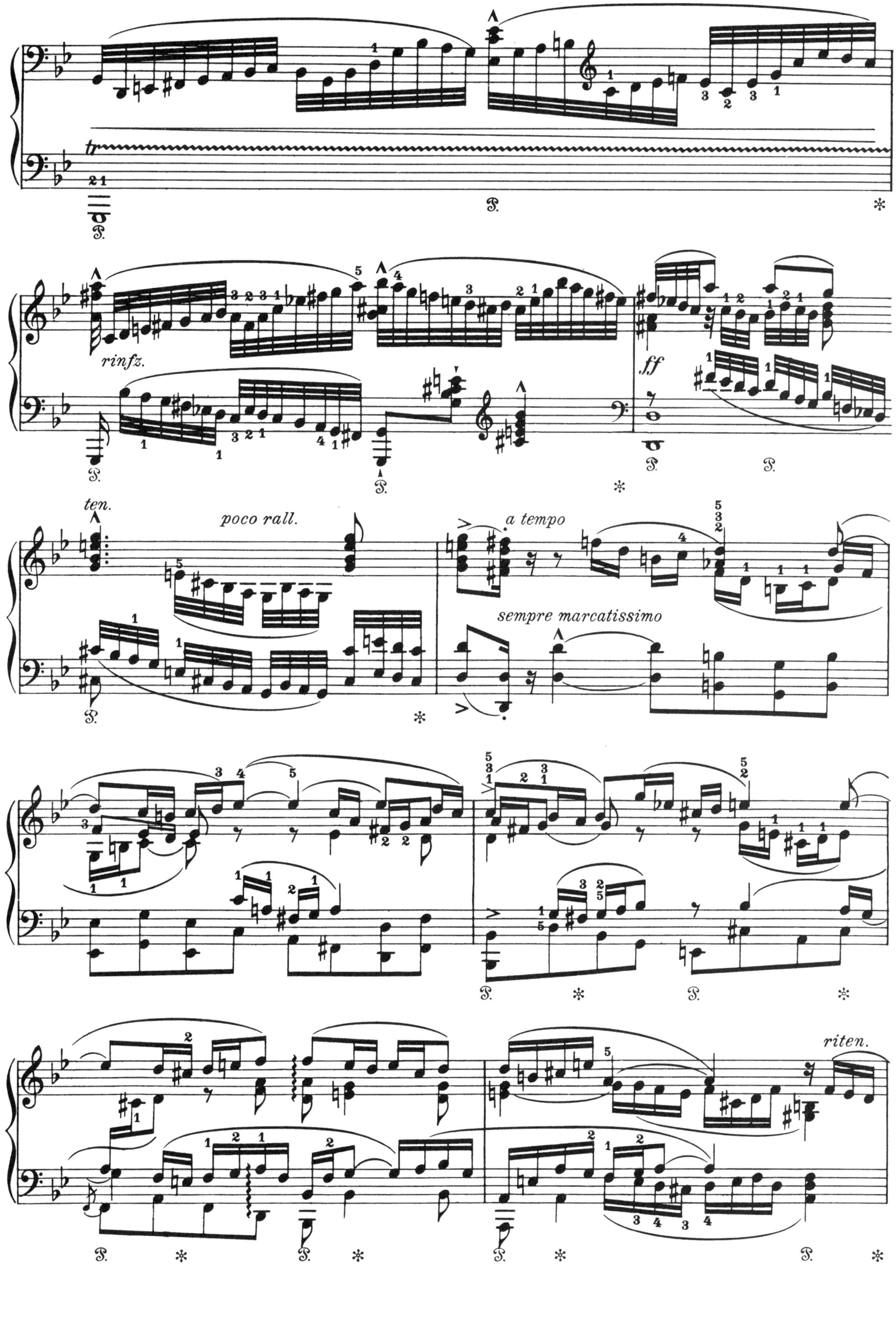
rinfz.
ff
ten.
poco rall.
a tempo
sempre marcatissimo
riten.

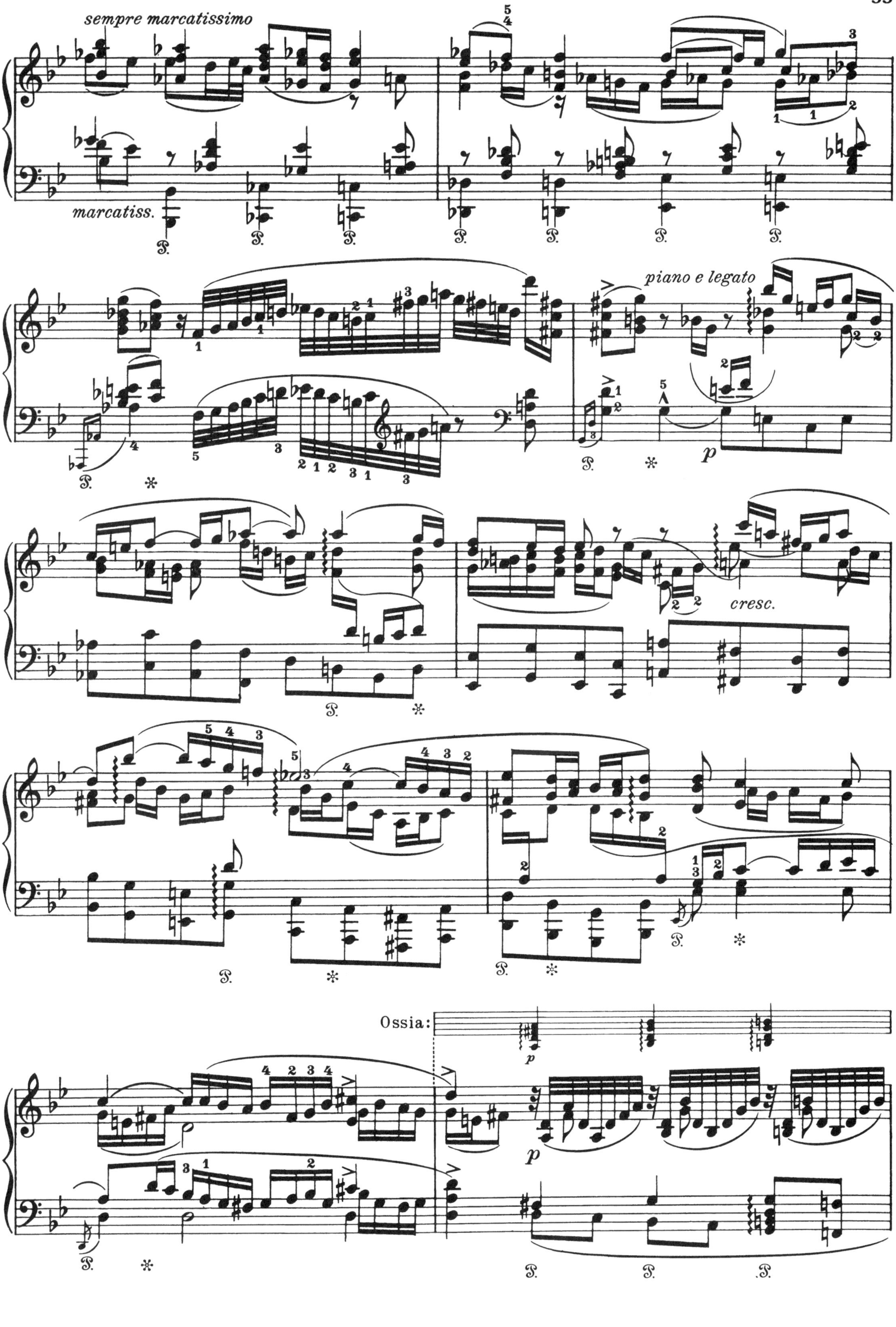
sempre marcatissimo
marcatiss.
piano e legato
p
cresc.
Ossia:
p
p

Fugue

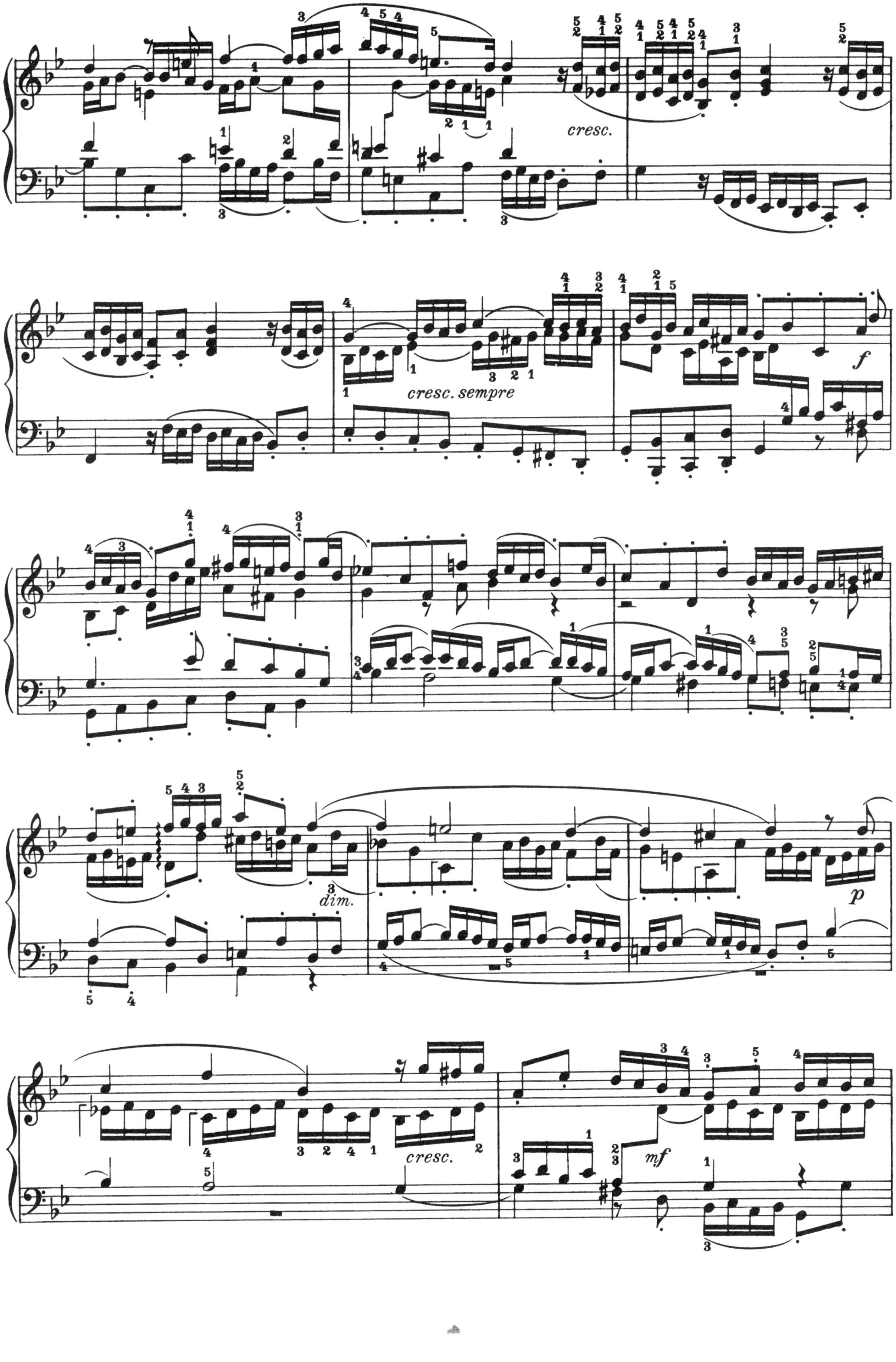
cresc.
cresc. sempre
f
dim.
p
cresc.
mf

GAVOTTE
from Sonata for Violin No. 2

Edited and fingered by Henry Levey

transcribed by Camille Saint-Saëns

ICH RUF ZU DIR, HERR
(I Call on Thee, Lord)

transcribed by Ferruccio Busoni

IN DIR IST FREUDE
(In Thee is Gladness)

transcribed by Ferruccio Busoni

JESUS BLEIBET MEINE FREUDE
(Jesu, Joy of Man's Desiring)
from Cantata No. 147

arranged by Wilhelm Kempff

*The transcriber omits the playing of the chorale at this place.

KOMM' SÜSSER TOD
(Come, Sweet Death)

arranged by Harold Bauer

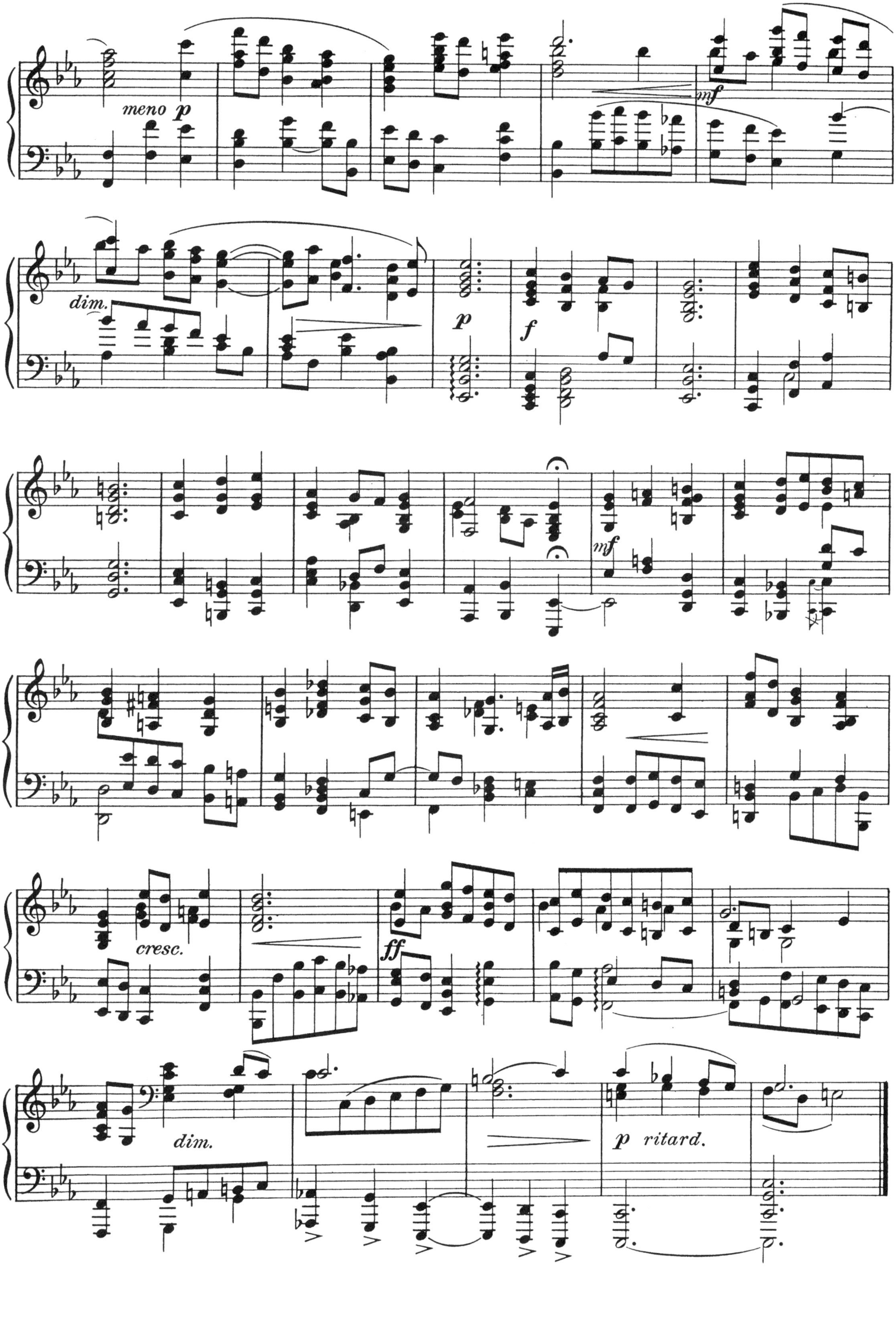
meno p
mf
dim.
p
f
mf
cresc.
ff
dim.
p ritard.

NUN FREUT EUCH, LIEBEN CHRISTEN
(Rejoice, Beloved Christians)

transcribed by Ferruccio Busoni

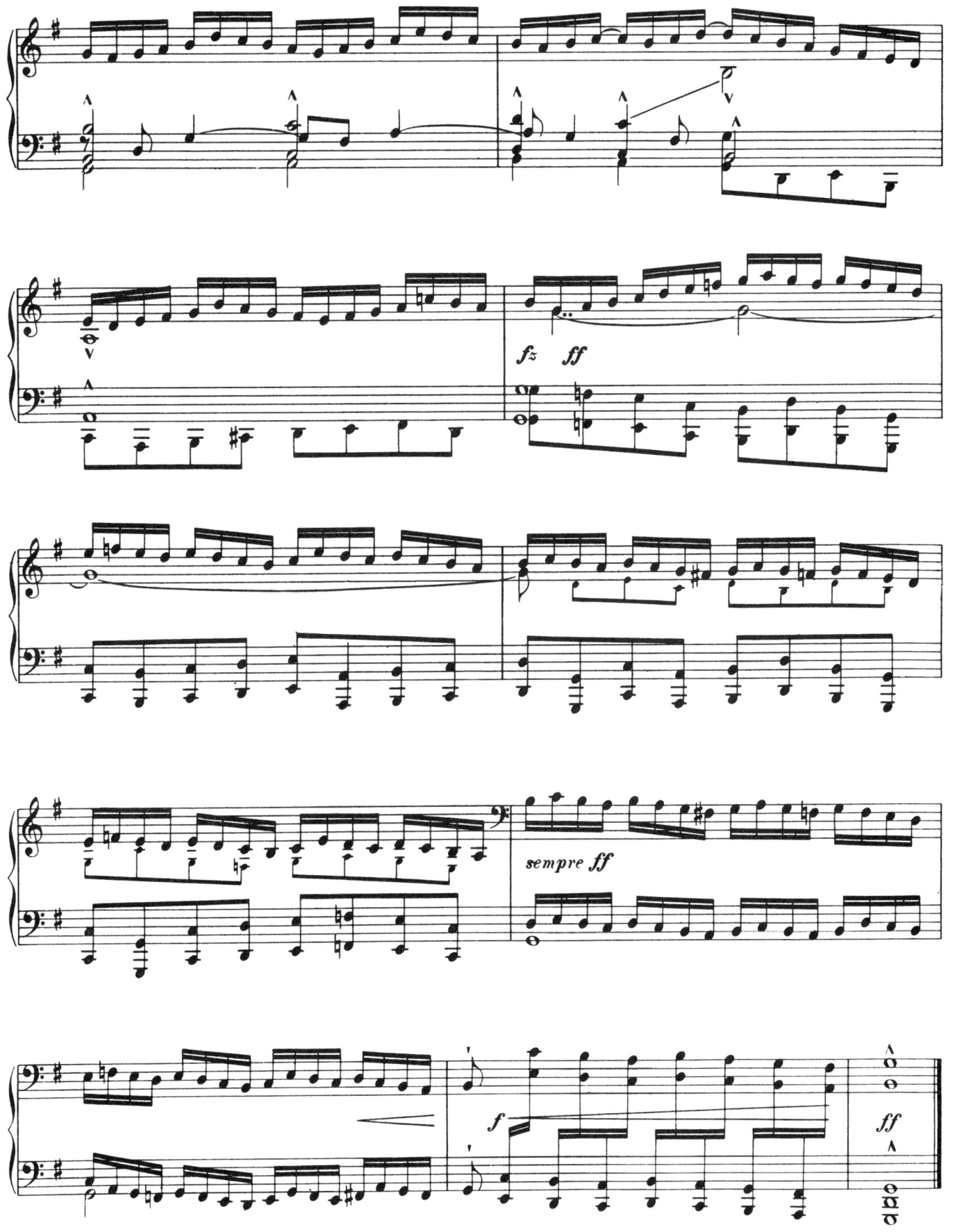

PRELUDE AND FUGUE
in A minor

arranged by Franz Liszt

Prelude

87

Fugue

96

PRELUDE AND FUGUE
in C major

Prelude

arranged by Franz Liszt

Fugue

Allegro maestoso

PRELUDE AND FUGUE
in D major

transcribed by Ferruccio Busoni

Prelude

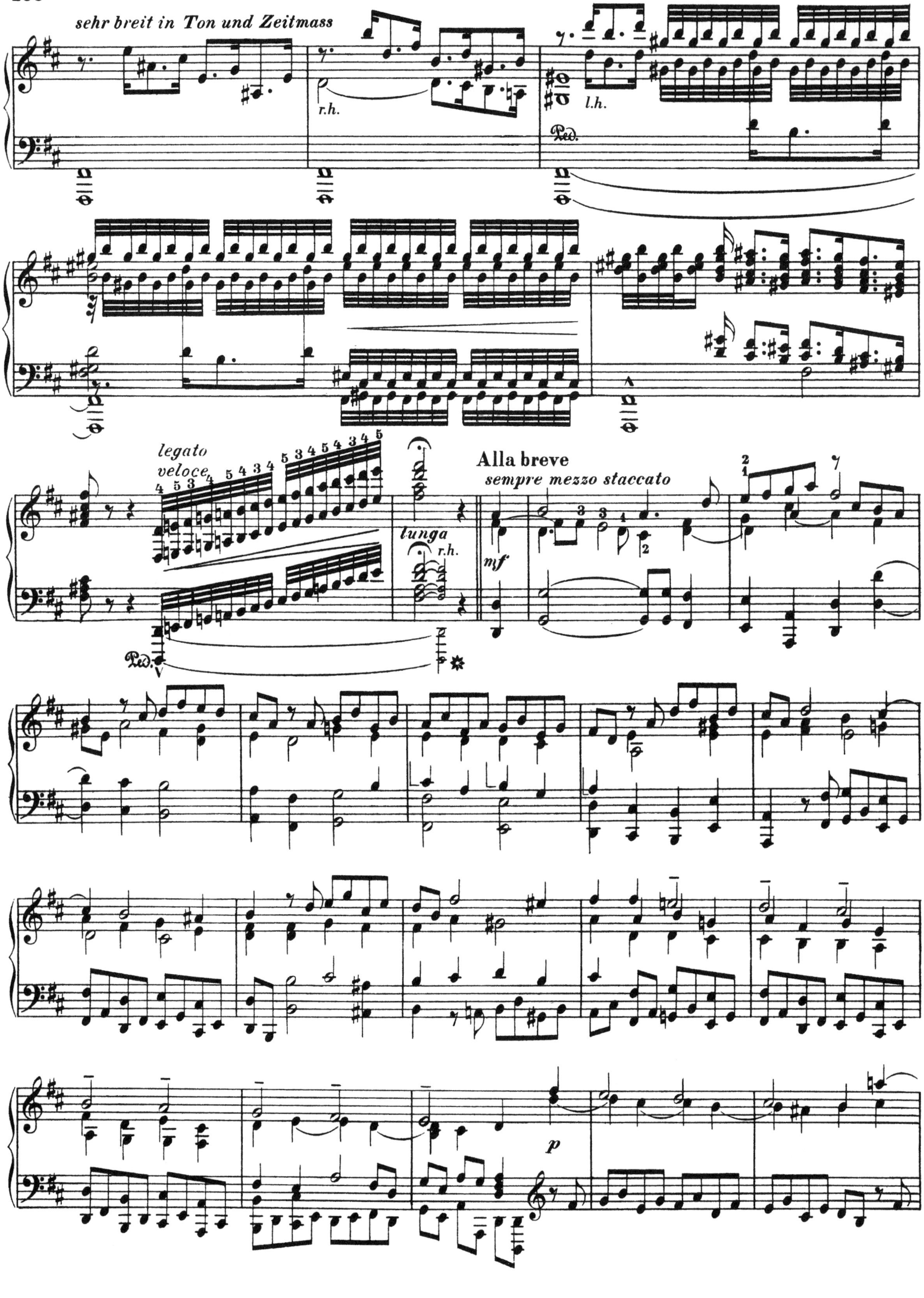
sehr breit in Ton und Zeitmass
r.h.
l.h.
Ped.
legato
veloce
lunga
r.h.
Ped.
Alla breve
sempre mezzo staccato
mf
p

PRELUDE AND FUGUE (St. Anne's)
in E♭ major

Prelude

transcribed by Ferruccio Busoni

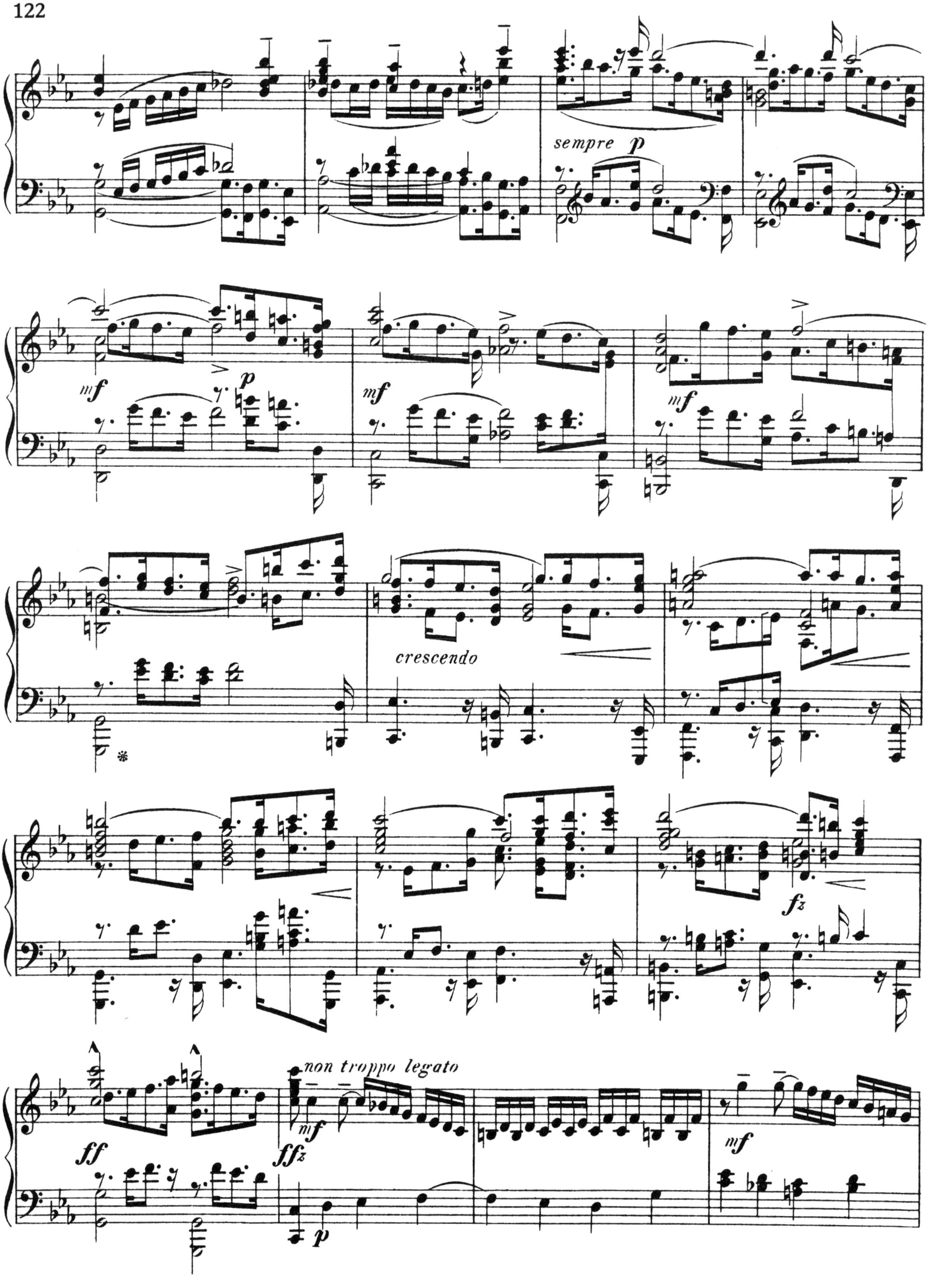
sempre p
mf
p
crescendo
fz
ff
ffz
non troppo legato

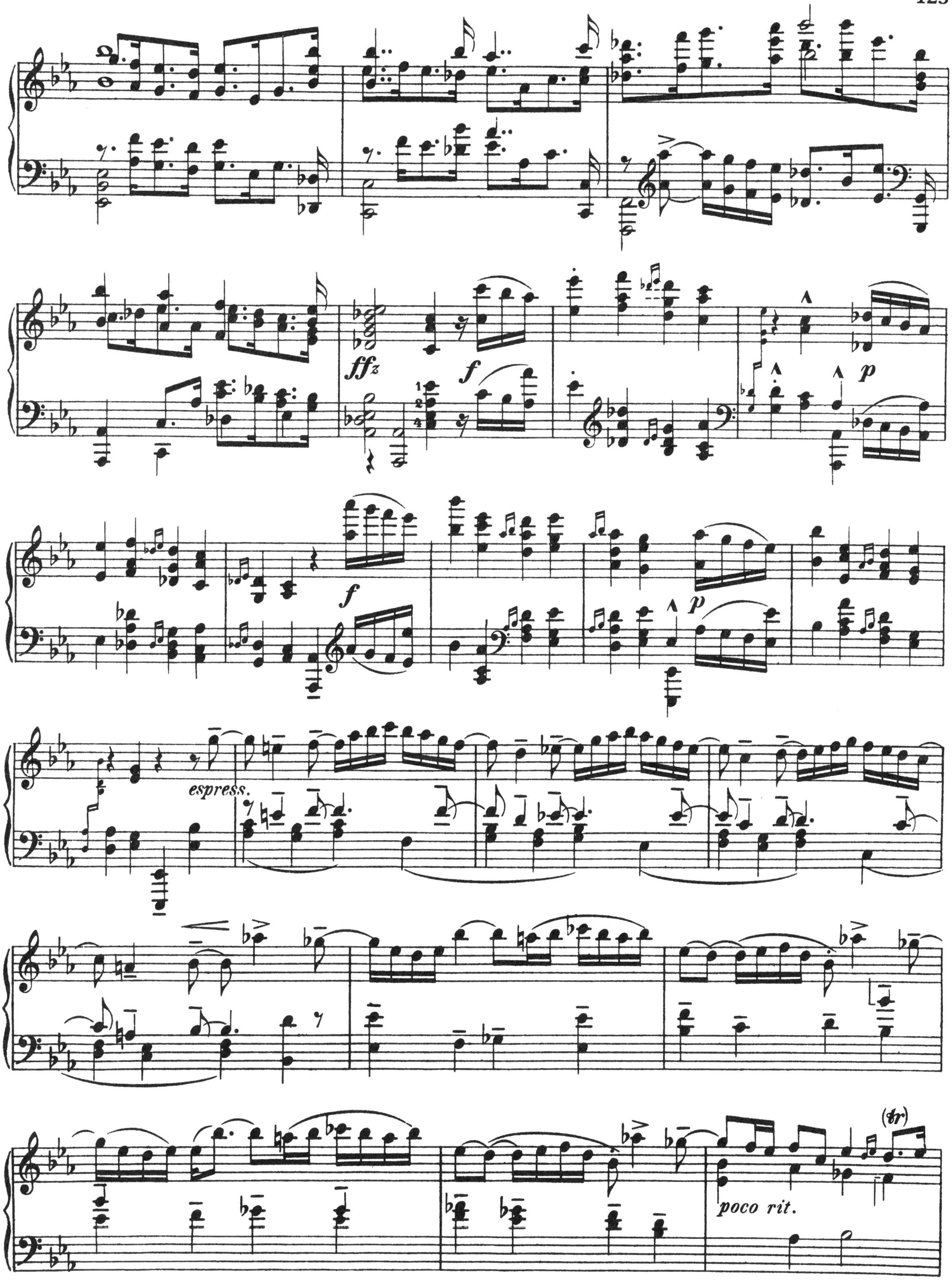
ffz
f
p
f
p
espress.
poco rit.
(tr)

Fugue

Allegro risoluto ed energico

PRELUDE AND FUGUE
in E minor

Prelude

arranged by Franz Liszt

Fugue

PRELUDE
from Partita in E major for Violin

Non Allegro

transcribed by Sergei Rachmaninoff

156

to Edwin Fischer
PRELUDE
to the Ratswahl Cantata

arranged by Wilhelm Kempff

To Albert Schweitzer

SICILIANO
from Flute Sonata No. 2

arranged by Wilhelm Kempff

PRESTO
after J.S. Bach

First Version

Johannes Brahms

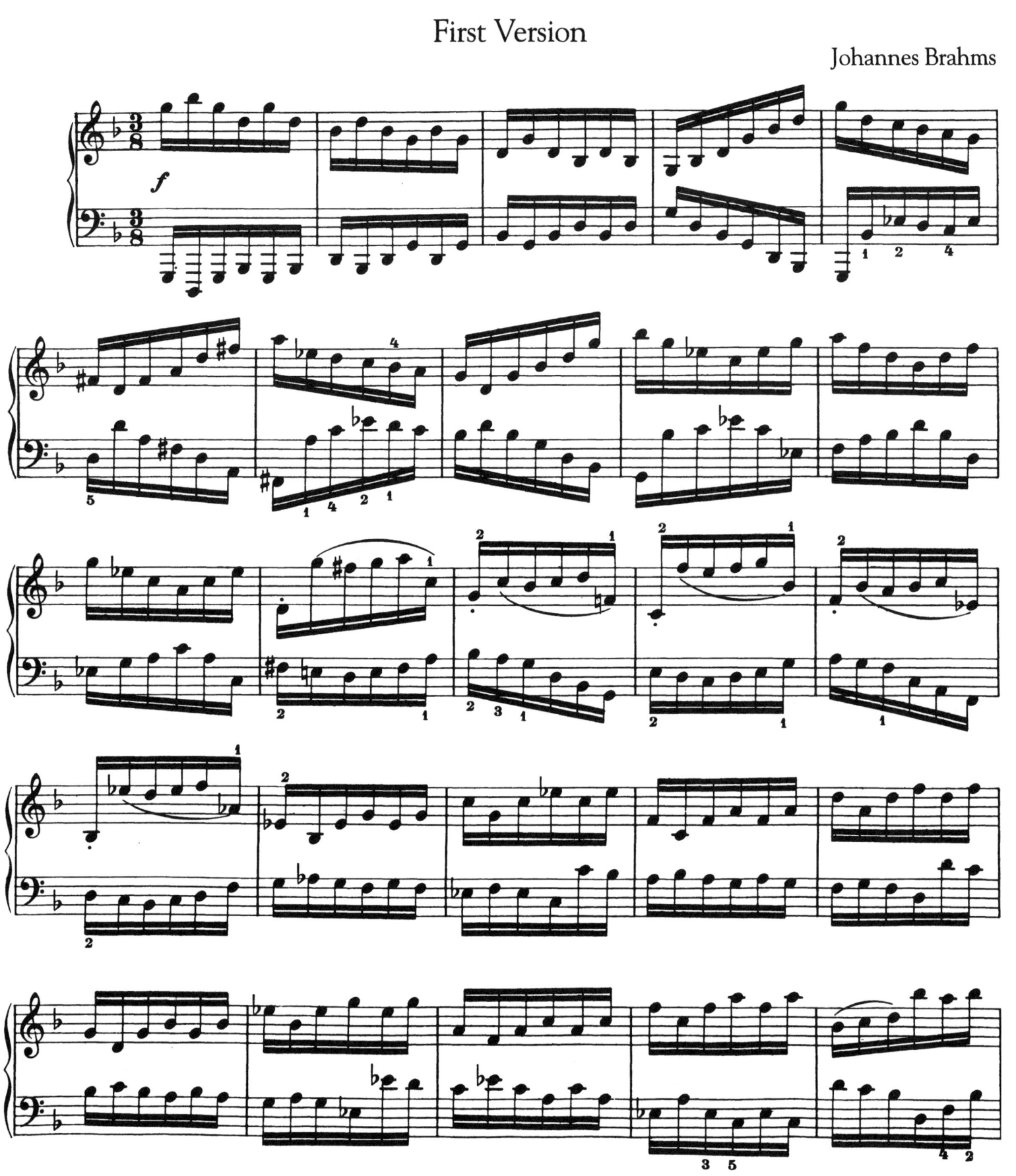

173

PRESTO
after J.S. Bach

Second Version

Johannes Brahms

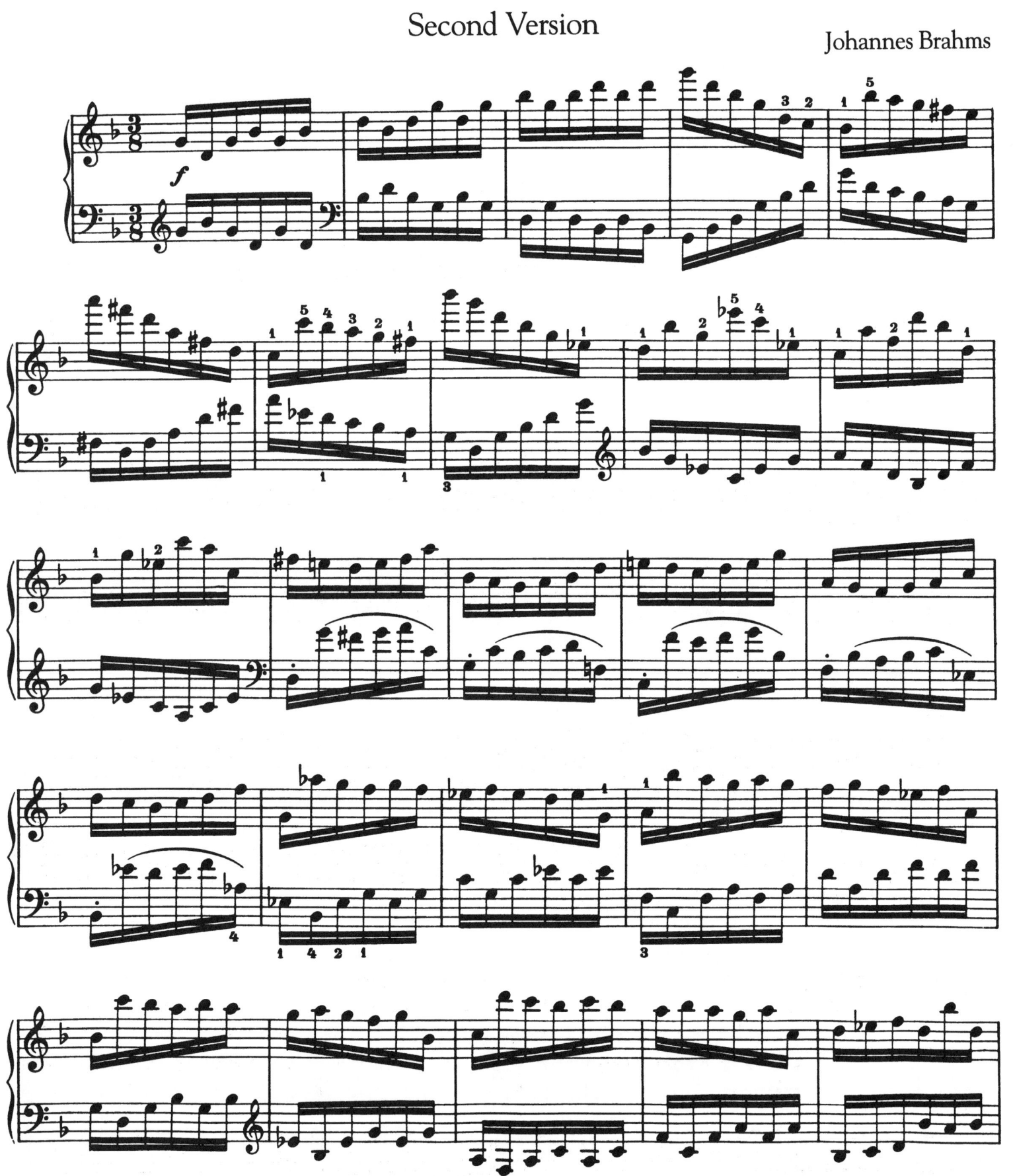

TOCCATA AND FUGUE
in C major

(**1. Preludio**, quasi improvvisando)
Tempo moderato

transcribed by Ferruccio Busoni

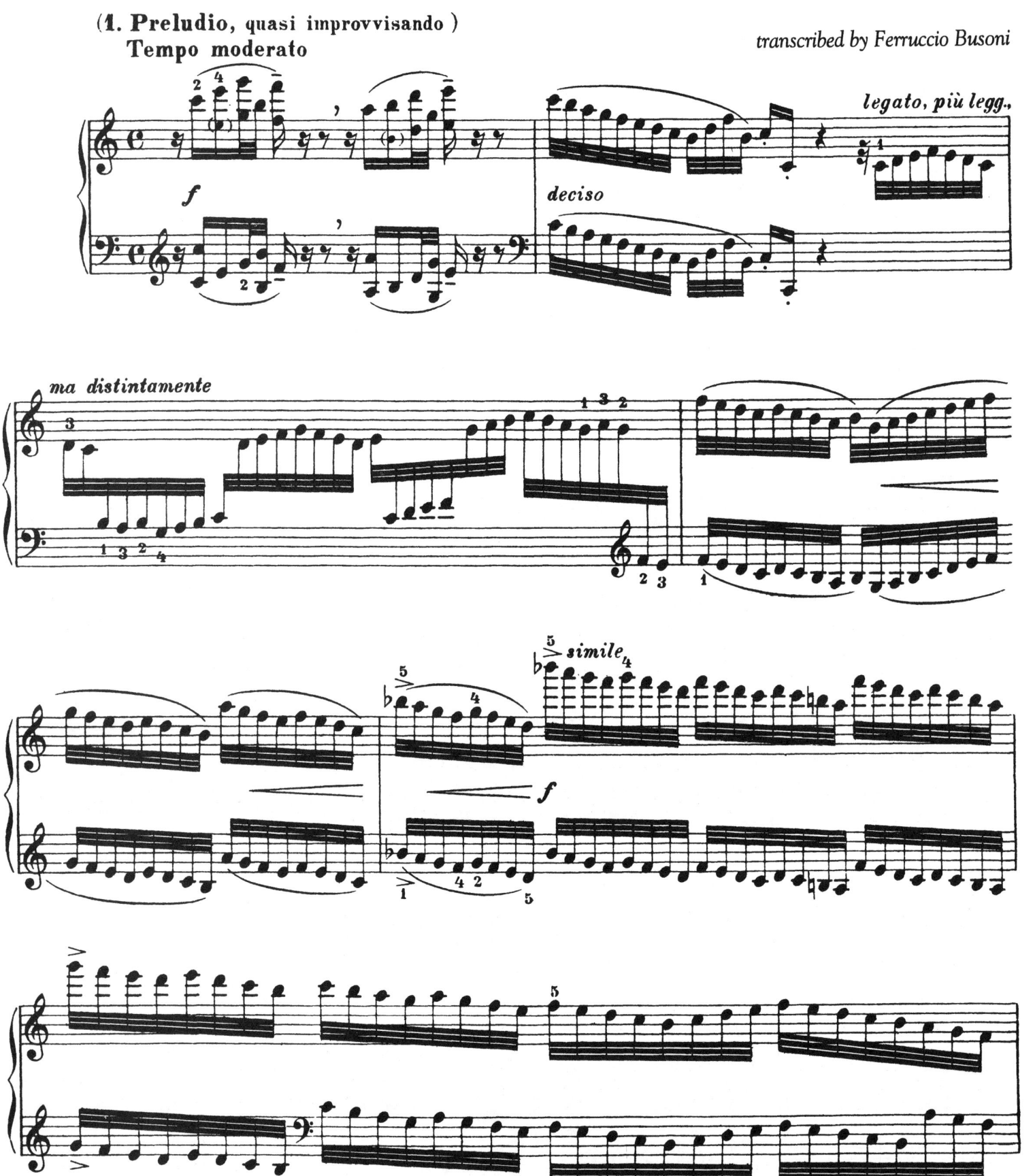

180

(molto misurato, senza espress. nè licenza alcuna)

182

(3. Fuga)

Moderatamente scherzando, un poco umoristico

mf marcato e con precisione, non legato

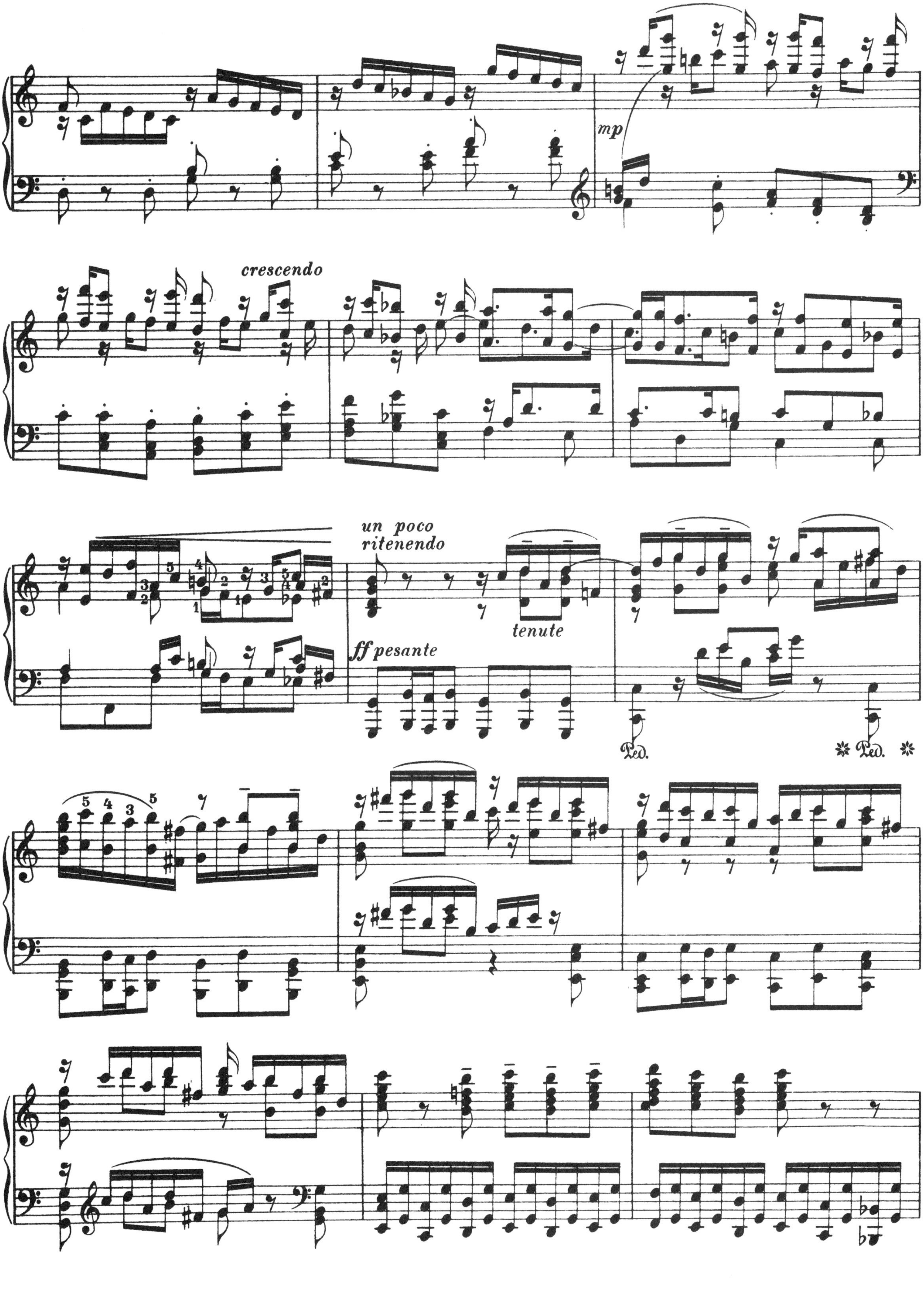
mp
crescendo
un poco
ritenendo
ff pesante
tenute
Ped.
Ped.

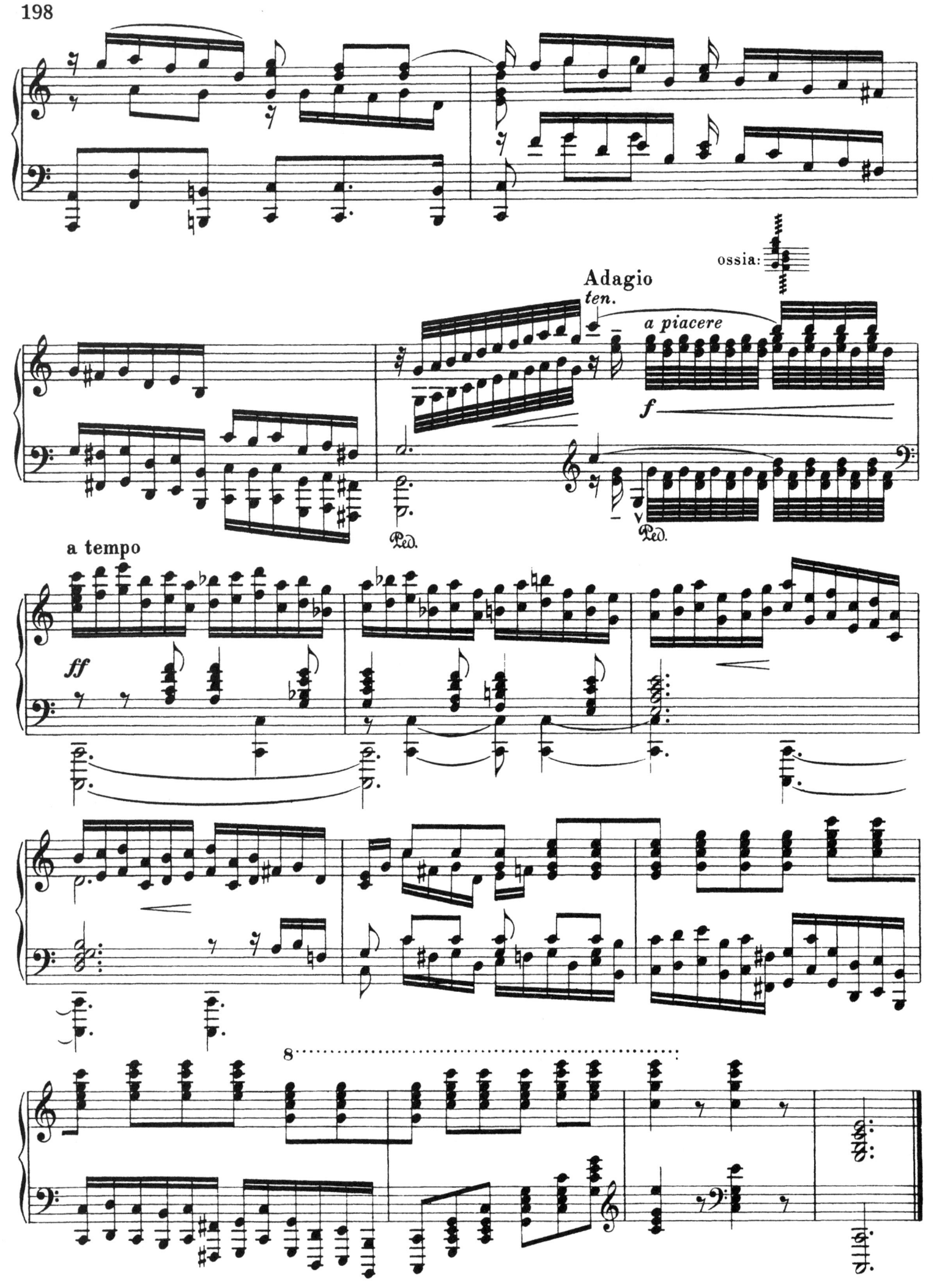

TOCCATA AND FUGUE
in D minor

transcribed by Ferruccio Busoni

Copyright © 1942 (renewed) by G. Schirmer, Inc. (ASCAP) New York, NY
International Copyright Secured. All Rights Reserved.
Warning: Unauthorized reproduction of this publication is
prohibited by Federal law and subject to criminal prosecution.

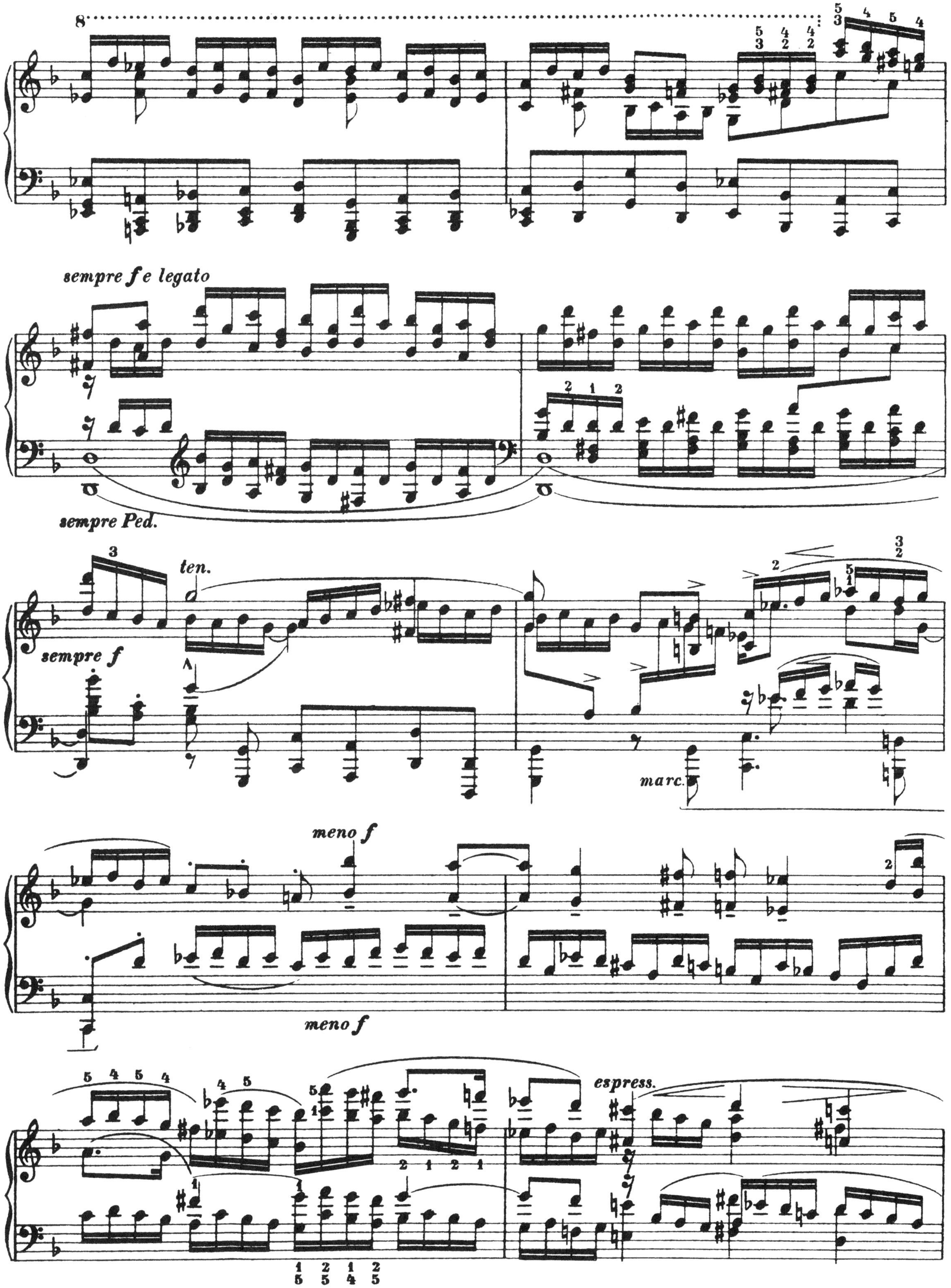
8
sempre f e legato
sempre Ped.
ten.
sempre f
marc.
meno f
meno f
espress.

WACHET AUF, RUFT UNS DIE STIMME
(Awake, the Voice Commands)

transcribed by Ferruccio Busoni

WACHET AUF, RUFT UNS DIE STIMME
(Awake, the Voice Commands)

arranged by Wilhelm Kempff